Signs of Life

a memoir in poems
by christina knowles

Signs of Life Copyright © 2016 by Christina Knowles.
All rights reserved. Printed in the United States of America. No part of this book may be used or reproduced in any manner whatsoever without written permission except in the case of brief quotations embodied in critical articles or reviews.
Book and cover design by Christina Knowles
Disturbing the Universe Publishing
For information contact: www.disturbingtheuniverseblog.com
ISBN: 978-0-692-79446-3

First Edition: October 2016
10 9 8 7 6 5 4 3 2 1

Signs of Life

a memoir in poems
by christina knowles

disturbing the universe publishing

For Randy, my biggest fan and constant source of encouragement. I love you.

Preface

I have always wanted to write my memoirs, the story of how I got from there to here. Perhaps, I just need to explain it to myself or to those I love. Perhaps, I need to leave a legacy for those who once knew me. At any rate, I find that whenever I try to express my deepest feelings and my most profound experiences, I do it through poetry, so here it is, my memoir in poems.

Table of Contents

Seeds	1
2 ½~Star Getaway	2
Christmas Lights	5
Because of You	6
Butterfly	10
Distant Trains	11
Dinner Party Queen	13
Dozens of Days and a Thousand Smiles	15
Falling	17
The Edge	19
Rede	21
Ashes	24
Free (#1)	26
Sisters	27
On a Cold November Day	29
Even in the Sunshine	30
When Love Had Just Begun	32
Lay Down My Arms	35
Transcend	37
I Remember You	40
Old Dogs	44
Flood	47
From Long Ago Dreams	48
Country	49
A Willow Bends	50
An Ocean of Possibility	51
Nothing's Ever Been the Same	52
A Voice Whispers	54
Helpless Anger	55
Questions	56
Trust	57
Entropy	58
A Caress from the Wind on the Sea	59

Endless Night	60
Music	67
No one can destroy you like a child	68
Signs of Life	70
Waiting for the Light	71
Rebellious by Nature	72
Married to You	73
The Sun Still Rises	74
In Memorium	76
I Know	78
Music Lives Here	81
Reversal	82
Those Eyes	83
Tossed	84
Black and White Promises	85
Art	86
Done	87
Breathe	88
Tomb	89
Honesty	90
Alone, I Thrive	92
Autumn	94
Fickle	95
I Grieve	97
Masterpiece	98
Bareback in the Meadow	99
Safe	101
I Dreamed of You Again Last Night	102
Free (#2, Letting Go)	104
Peaceful Harbor	106
Apprentice	107
Book Tribe	108
Stop the World	110
Remembering	111
Transformed	112
Escape	113
The Stone	115

The Broken Become Wise 116
Teacher 118
Snow Day 120
Words Don't Fail Me 121
Little dog 122
Bohemian Atheist 124
Just Gone 126
All the Heaven and Hell 128
Lucky 130
Morning Light 132
Alive 133
Appendix
About the Author
Also by Christina Knowles

Seeds

I ate of watermelon sweet.
I barely chewed its pulp as it—
It slid along my throat so slick,
Like water sliding off a rock,
Its smoothness trickled down my neck.
I sucked its juice and tasted life—
A slice of pale red paradise.
Inhaling breaths between large bites,
I choked upon a little seed—
A small black spot—reality.

2 ½~Star Getaway

Get away!
Retreat
to the big white screen,
my tranquil Nevis—
where the steamiest scenes
soothe the senses.
Tropical chick-flick?
Damen or Pitt covered in sand,
a swirling mai-tai in hand, randomly out of sync
with the rest of creation.

What? Tired of Sex on the Beach?
Let's eat!
To the Caribbean for the treasure of chicken noodle
salad.
And for dessert—Depp
or a little danger, Hollywood style.
An adventure or two? To Prague,
should you choose to accept
the risky appeal of Classic Cruise—
always a winner with an impossible mission.

Meanwhile, concentrate.
Unbore yourself,

unbore!

How about an Irish escapade?
The Haunting and heart-rending,
dark and stormy nights
in cathedralish greenhouses,
and in the closing sequence,
a mad rush of precarious acrophobia—
high above gross sculptures and spiral staircases.

Or maybe something educational?
Baryshnikov is beautiful this time of year.
Ballet, anyone?
Anyone?
First position—perfectly contracted?
It's all in the name of patriotism.
No disavowal or defection,
until the second reel.

But wait! Sneak a peak
next door,
where the undefeatable meet the diabolical.
Swanky, sly women
dressed in red,
the unseen evil
of six-inch-heel-seductions.
Then, maniacally,
they burst their brains in a horror film—

How unoriginal,
yet strangely edifying.

Christmas Lights

These stars that blink and chase entice my mind.
I stare as plastic people dance and turn
On mirrored ice to silent songs behind
A frosted glass. The candles wax and burn.
My eyes—hypnotized, dazed by lights that churn
And swirl, a flick'ring glow, while shadows fall
Around the tiny room. The taciturn
Snowflakes drop slow and heavy. They enthrall
Me as I gaze, unmoving through the tall
And lighted buildings of the street. I wake
Up from my reverie and tug my shawl
A little tighter now. The last snowflake
Has fallen from my view, and so I turn
To go. Life is awaiting my return.

Because of You

I've always looked up to you
It was so easy to do
My life is so wrapped up with you

You stayed home with me
When I was sick, you comforted me tenderly
You kept me quiet on Christmas mornings
With stories of Santa and gentle warnings
I remember late night stories on your bed
To Adventure Land you led
To a world of imagination
Your words an invitation
I read everything you gave me
A new world opened gaily
Science fiction, fantasy
Suspense, a genre tapestry

I always looked up to you
My life was so wrapped up in you

I listened to you play your flute
In your room, music took root
You gave me records that I still have
Tchaikovsky, Mozart, and Chopin
You introduced to me to culture I never would've had
It's because of you, I'm who I am
You took to me to buy my first good skates
You listened all about my first dates

Listened to my teenage angst
Put up with all my juvenile pranks
You let me come and stay with you
Just what I needed; I guess you knew

It was so easy to do
Looking up to you

You bought my prom dress, so I wouldn't miss the event
Then you managed to get Mom's consent
Always on my side it seems
You supported all my dreams
Tutored me and never disdained
The hours, the concepts explained
You co-signed for my first credit
Trusted me; I'm forever indebted
When I went away, you took care of my dog
Every week, you read my blog
You went with me to *Star Trek* club meetings
Conventions, outings, and club proceedings

My entire life is intertwined with you
I am who I am because of you

All through our lives we've had such good times
Remember when we went to Disney and stood in those lines?
We screamed all the way down Splash Mountain
Took our picture in front of the fountain
Universal Studios was such a blast
That trip went way too fast
A Hawaiian luau, taking in the show

An earthquake, a flood, just Hollywood though
We haven't taken a trip like that in a while
Now days, it's more our style
Dinner and a movie on Friday nights
It's still one of my favorite rites

It's no wonder I look up to you
My life is so infused with you

The holidays we always share together
Thanksgiving at my house, no matter the weather
Christmas at yours and candlelight service
The Living Christmas tree and your performance
Playing the bells on Christmas Eve
Christmas dinner, and after— a movie
Sometimes A *Christmas Carol*
Or we'd see *The Nutcracker Ballet*
In our finest apparel
A *Christmas Story* once again we'd replay
Our traditions are so special to me
Sisters, but friends, especially

My life is so wrapped up with you
It's easy to look up to you

A chemist, a musician, an intellect to admire
An older sister, a height to aspire
A friend and a confidant
You went way beyond
What a sister should be
What a friend could see
I'll always look up to you

It's so easy to do
Because my life is wrapped up with you
And I am who I am because of you

Butterfly

Lightly, wings flutter
Warm rays dance on thin black legs
Softly, Butterfly

Distant Trains

Though miles apart, the same blood runs through our veins
On different tracks, we wave, riding gracious trains
A big brother and a little sister, two branches on the family tree
Through time and space, you linger in my memory

Images of you from childhood wane
Faded pictures lovingly explain
A Christmas wish book and a Santa story
A moment in time, but not transitory

Because no matter the miles, our blood is the same
Idolized, a big brother contains
The wisdom and sweetness of reverie
Looking up to a you, a brotherly apogee

Distant the miles, but our blood is the same
We took separate paths, but love remains
Older, you spent your life far from me
Pursuing your dreams separately

Through the miles, our blood remains
But on different tracks, we wave, riding distant trains
We smile wistfully
Sharing a memory

At times, we gather to reminisce, too often in pain

Through time and distance, love is the chain
But in sorrow, we pull together as family
In joy, we share transiently

Because the same blood runs through our veins
And we're never gone so long as to constrain
The feelings between you and me
Two branches on the family tree

Though miles apart, blood sustains
And on different tracks, riding distant trains
We smile and wave wistfully
Sharing the same sweet memories

Dinner Party Queen

Entering your enormous and lovely apartment,
you greet me with your gratuitous smile,
your plastic-flower image, and oh-so-courteous
temperament.
You taunt me with your high-styled manners
and your generous remarks snub me as they normally do.
"How do you take your Beluga?" and "Which wine do
you prefer?"
and "Oh, I didn't mean to assume—I'll be happy to select
for you."
You quickly explain to all of your friends
my regrettable shortcomings and beg them to forgive
my sinful lack of politesse, and then
politely excuse yourself and float across the room,
leaving me blundering in your cultural forum.
As I bitterly gaze at your perfect state,
your fashionable clothing gaily stabs me in the back—
your mission in life, so-to-speak.
Crimson faced, I hate to admit
your silky silhouette does look stupendous
in your A-line frock and jacaranda-dyed heels.
I would never say it conflicts with your artistically
painted face,
contrasting so vibrantly your pale complexion.
Bullhorn-bright and swelling with pride,
you sweep through the room, bulldozing my dignity
with your swanky attire and arrogant demeanor.
Slowly, I slide away from the circle of beautiful people

and fade into the paisley wallpaper,
which, I might add, is out of style.
Here I blend.
Again, I gaze in your direction,
your elegant coiffure turns up its nose at my violin-string hair.
Mortified, I hide
humbly in the corner reserved for shopping school dropouts.
Slouching behind your ornate décor,
I look down at my flower-flocked frock and Payless shoes,
and ponder my sanity—why did I come?
I really must control these masochistic tendencies.
Swallowing down my caustic remorse; emerging
I slither my worm body over to your graceful self
and settle at your satin shoes.
Weakly, I rise up through the ashes of my incinerated pride
and face your rude disposition.
"Although it's been so lovely, I really must be going,"
I croak as I meet your captivating blue eyes with my insipid ones.
"Before dinner? Oh well, if you must,"
you drawl so gallantly, perceiving your work is complete,
and I may again return to my hovel, properly placed.
Recognizing the dominance of your station, I retreat.
Backing down from the challenge, I fall into line
at the prosaic end of the pecking order.
There really was never any debate.

Dozens of Days and a Thousand Smiles

Dozens of days in my memory play
I can't help but smile
Rewinding the slow serenity of those days
Reflecting on each fleeting mile
Each ephemeral year that goes by
The collected hours, passed time
The unfortunate distance we multiply
That priorities realign
Separated by a thousand small details
As time seems to stretch before us without end
We can't quite make out all it entails
And what lies around each future bend
But I remember those days when
We could just sit for awhile
Sipping coffee or talking and then
Fishing on a still mountain lake
Camping at Eleven Mile
Swapping stories in the break
While time stretched before us without end
The wind blowing through my hair
Speeding through turns
On the back of your bike, unaware
Of time slipping by, unconcerned
I remember driving cross-country in the snow
Holding our breath through the pass
A little CCR on the stereo
Rubbing the frost from the glass
As time stretched before us without end

Just watching westerns on a lazy Saturday afternoon
Nothing but time to spend
I never realized life would move on so soon
I remember when you taught me to drive
And how to work on cars, to prep and to sand
Working together, talking and laughing comprised
Our minutes and hours, a lifetime spanned
Leaving me with a thousand smiles
Memories to tend
Images of dozens of days and hundreds of miles
As time stretches behind us without end

Falling

As clouds race by and time stands still,
Images float and wax surreal.
English sonnets plummet down from castle tops.
Below, a dense grey fog shrouds a blue-green copse.
Misty mountains that loom overhead
Cast their shadows of morbid dread.
Crooked steps lead to lies and deception—
I lose my way in a sea of obsession.
I walk with the dead on a sandy beach
As apparitions melt and spirits leach.
The air hangs on me like a velvet drape;
The drawbridge is up and I can't escape.
Terror envelopes me in soft, dark clouds
And lingers over my burial shrouds.
Clean, breaking waves crash over my coffin.
Dissolving the stones, my bed they soften.
Sliding, crashing, shattering my locks.
Slippery fingers grab at the rocks.
Jagged cliffs scream at the sky,
Climbing crags dang'rously high.
Rugged rocks rip open my gown,
Tearing flesh, plunging me down.
Falling and flying through salt-water air,
Screaming and scratching feeds my nightmare.
Falling forever, eternally sleep,
Grotesque reflections in waters so deep.
Watery grave swallowed and sealed
Revels in dark secrets revealed.

Souls possessed coveted no more
Dream only to rest—evermore.

The Edge

Linear lives stumble past
each other
in blind obedience
to an unknown god—
money, possessions,
success.
Occasionally we meet—
our eyes, our bodies.
Rarely ourselves.
But today I am with you,
and your delicate flesh gives way to my touch.
Entangling limbs,
need fuses us together.
Sweat drips like tears down our bodies,
cleansing our souls,
washing away rivers of indifference,
momentarily.
I am connected to you in this instant.
We seem to be one, our souls speaking a secret language.
Occasionally we meet—
our eyes, our flesh.
Sometimes ourselves.
Waves of sensation subside with the tide.
Relief flows evenly across our bodies like summer wind.
I emerge less than whole, transformed;
already retreating into my separate self.
Our bodies touch,
but there are miles between us.

Your heavy weight presses me down,
smothering my humanity,
turning me into another
in an endless procession of animal-like
bodies, soulless.
Occasionally we meet—
our eyes, our flesh.
Why not ourselves?
We are separate
until
we once again find that common ground
with each other
or someone else.
This newly born awareness grows
while emotion fades
away—like an old man breathing his last.
Lingering
on the edge of bliss,
on the edge of emptiness
Until that day when we finally meet
Ourselves.

Rede

Live in peace and harmony
The Old Way states
To each his own and blesséd be
To none her vengeance lay; the three-fold law awaits
Count the stars, neighbors to the waning moon
Widdershins go until she turns
Whispering the ancient rune
While in the fire, nine woods burn
Casting shadows upon a wall
Stir the elements with the knife
Sweep away mischief's bitter gall
Draw upon her force of life
Deosil go when she waxes full
The circle three times cast
And on the lady mull
Libations offer, wine in glass
And elder be the lady's tree, reaching
To the ancient goddess
Beseeching
As all life watches
Arms stretched in wonder
The wind sings his plea
Kindness to us all under
The ancient oaken tree
Share in her loving motherhood
For we are one upon the earth
From the willow wood
To the river's bubbling mirth

Toss the stone and find
Truth where the rippling waters flow
Merry meet and merry part, kind
Wherever we may go
And harm ye none, do what you will with ever an open heart.

Ashes

He thinks he knows me
He imagines he understands the storm
Inside
But he's never observed the chaos of the wind
The beauty of truth
Only a black and white score card
Bullet points on a sheet of paper
Results of a disaster
He's never felt the force of the rain driving
Inside.

He thinks he understands what's going on
But the storm goes unnoticed
Until lightning strikes too close
Igniting the tattered edges of hope
Incinerating the slightest remnant of regard
Still oblivious to destruction
Stumbling on, tripping over the fallen pieces of me
Denying the devastation

He thinks he knows me
But I'm not sure we've even met
Who I am does not matter
When it comes to damage control
He's witnessed the evidence—
Seen our simulated lives shredded and charred,
Like entries in a diary, burning in a fire.
Reality is not regarded

He thinks he can control the outcome
Cool the blaze that has yet gone unchecked
Find a treaty
In the ashes that remain
Revive the breath in us

Finally, he recognizes death
He sees it in my eyes—
Fogged over with rose petals and lined with satin
As I unknowingly drift through people and days
He stares at the ground
As he smashes the embers into the cold earth
But in the ash, a seed
begins to germinate—
New life, me
Independent and strong
And gloriously alone

Free (#1)

To be suddenly liberated by my own hands
Is the purest joy
Lightness fills me
With every clean, icy breath
For the first time
Free
Tearing the tethers from my limbs
I run on open ground
I cannot see the end
Only infinite panoramas
Every possibility stretching before me
Twilight emerges, but darkness is hours away
There is time
Even a moment is enough
To exist in my own skin
To decide every detail
To roll playfully in the grass
And shout my true thoughts to the universe
Refusing ever to be muted
Once colorless and paper-thin
Each day a pretense
Quietly placating
I caught myself on the brink of death
And revived myself
Breathed in a new life
I am my own savior
Now I live
Free

Sisters

Paper dolls
Cut from a magazine
Little girl dreams
Played out in scenes
Pretending to be characters from
Land of the Giants, I'd be one—
Valerie; you'd be the other—Betty
You were a little older
But still we'd conspire over
Elvis movies and Barbies
Disagreeing hardly
Six years apart in one room together
Whether a pleasure or a conflict of space
Romance novels and baby dolls shared the place
Love was the tether, family the base
I begged you to play
You didn't seem to mind
A fray or two, we drew the line
In tape across the floor
Dividing space, restoring rapport
My big sister adoring
I tagged along, questions forming
You rarely ignoring
Me in favor of teenage things
A patience that loyalty brings
As years pass like hours
Memories gain their power
Like running through a sprinkler on a summer day

A weekend stowaway
In a college dorm
Lunch dates and movie nights
An adult friendship formed
Days spent scrapbooking
And family invites
Talking and laughing
Memories amassing
Because a teenage you knew what it would mean
To nurture the unseen
The kindness to attend
To a little sister, a small friend
Always concerned, admiration earned
You were always a compassionate caretaker
Memory-maker
On your loyalty and love
I continually depend,
A little sister who always called you a friend.

On a Cold November Day

On a cold November day, the family's all at home
The young, the old, the in-between
Gathered 'round the table where the love we feel is known

Elbow to elbow, at the table we've outgrown
We pass the traditional cuisine
On a cold November day with the family all at home

The clattering of the dishes, the warm chaotic tone
It's always the same beautiful routine
Gathered 'round the table where the love we feel is shown

The smell of sage and cinnamon, satiety we bemoan
Still we pass the dishes, endless fare it seems
On a cold November day when the family's all at home

Napping on the sofa, Grandpa snores and groans
While a Christmas movie plays on the TV screen
We've gathered 'round the fire where the love we feel is known

The bantering and the laughing, the joyful overtone
Grouping for a photo, capturing the scene
On a cold November day with the family all at home
Gathered 'round the fire where the love is always known

Even in the Sunshine

I have looked at my life through a scarred and dusky glass
and longed for it to end,
and I have known the splendor of the ordinary
and prayed for time to spend.

I've choked back the tears,
then let them fall like rain.
I've reveled in my sorrow,
and I've laughed and smiled
and known the bliss of breathing,
looking forward to tomorrow.

I've let the emptiness invade me.
I've felt the loss of those who've gone,
Turned to You for comfort,
wallowed in Your love,
and I've woken to see the dawn.

I've felt love swell inside me
and lost sight of You in joy;
the source of it was blurred.
I've forgotten You in beauty
and relished all Your blessings
without a single word.

And I have suffered loss and praised You
and blessed Your name in my despair.
I've clung to You in grief

and never questioned the pain I've had to bear.

And I've known joy in sorrow,
surrendered to Your peace.
I have thrilled in all Your blessings
and thanked You without cease.
I've held them loosely in my hand
and turned to You in gladness,
not only in my pain.
I've remembered You in joy
and needed You in gain.

I've seen the change in me through misery;
I've seen the change in my delight.
I've learned to need You in the sunshine,
just as I need You through the night.

When Love Had Just Begun

I never knew love like
Turtles in a bucket
A Big Wheel racing down the street
And Crash Dummies on concrete
Like Stretch Armstrong with arms three-feet long
Like Legos and Lincoln Logs
And dinosaurs on the lawn

I never knew love like
Pumpkin patches in autumn
And sledding on snow days
Or pancakes on delays
Like sipping homemade cocoa
While putting up the tree
And cookies for Santa on Christmas Eve

I never knew love like
Cowboy boots and badges, a toy gun on the hip
Hockey sticks and skates
And Indiana's whip
Like tickle fights and taunting
Begging for no more
And laughing till we're sore

I never knew love like
Airsoft and Super Soakers
In the summer sun
Like climbing rocks and biking

Muddy shoes and hiking
Like scary stories 'round the campfire
Like grass stains and board games while it rains

I never knew love like
Movie nights and pizza
Like *Young Guns* on the screen
And video games in between
Like a picnic on a blanket
Right on the living room floor
Mario Cart and *Halo*, fighting for high score

I never knew love like
Sandboxes and swimming pools
Garages strewn with tools,
Golf clubs, and hockey gear
And cars retrofitted every year
With fins and chrome exhaust
On a Chevy Cavalier

I never knew love like
A newborn son
Like a blonde-haired boy
Loved by everyone
A caring brother
Humorous and sheltering
Generous and affectionate

Like a loving father
Benevolent, protective
Kind and attentive
Like a husband to a wife

Treating her with care
Grown responsible in life
Working hard to provide

I never knew love like
That of a mother for a child
The definition of unconditional
Memories compiled
I never knew love like
The longing for my son
Reflections of a time when love had just begun

Lay Down My Arms

Should I lay down my arms and surrender?
Should I fall at Your feet and be still?
Can I be overwhelmed by Your splendor
And bent to Your heavenly will?

I'm a wave tossed in an ocean of doubt
Tormented and torn, I resist and defy
Acknowledge the truth I can't do without
Or harden my heart, Your goodness deny?

Do I deny You with my lips
When my heart may believe
Betray You with a kiss
And refuse to receive?

If I should lay down my arms and surrender
Fall at Your feet and be still
Can I be overwhelmed by Your splendor
And bent to Your heavenly will?

And when You, I inevitably betray
Cursing, crucifying with my pride
Will You close your ears, or hear me pray?
Will You call my name, arms open wide?

Will Your patience last till the end of my days
Though I turn my back, continually ignore
Your mercy, Your grace, the question You raise

Your sacrifice, Your death, my sin that You bore?

Should I lay down my arms and surrender?
Should I fall at Your feet and be still?
Can I be overwhelmed by Your splendor
And bent to Your heavenly will?

Transcend

Did you ever wonder
About the trees, the flowers, and the seas?
Not just to use and plunder,
Thinking we are so much more than these?

Did you ever wander
Through the forest of many creatures rife?
Did you stop to ponder
In the night, what animal builds his life?

Did you ever ponder
The living, the breathing of everything around?
The flutter of feathered wings, the sacred honor
Of crunching leaves of scarlet scattered on the ground?

Do you ever wonder
What the sleeping dog dreams?
Is he chasing squirrels in a field over yonder?
Is he romping through crystal clear streams?

Does the elephant love her child
Stolen from her care?
Chained and defiled
She mourns her loss with a tear.

Did you ever wonder
Why humans feel superior?
Stripping lands and torturing under

The belief that all else is inferior?

Do you feel the need to plunder,
Destroying forests to supply
The cities of man? We tear asunder,
Building skyscrapers to pierce the sky.

Do we worship the ability to destroy?
We talk about intelligence;
It's just a clever ploy
To justify our negligence and squander Earth's inheritance.

Why do we build a pedestal, and climb into the seat,
Claiming we have a soul, and other beasts do not?
Privy to the secrets of an afterlife replete
In rewards for destruction with their blood we bought?

Do we ever wonder
Why we're comfortable with our thoughts
Of eternal days unnumbered
While they turn to dust in their plots?

Did we ever consider
We are one and the same?
Energy reconfigured,
Just another creature's frame?

Born of the earth,
Siblings of the land
With no separate worth;

No destiny is planned.

Did you ever wonder
If it's time to transcend?
Wake up from this slumber
And begin to comprehend?

We are all a part of another,
So end the devastation, and instead defend
Those at our hands who suffer
And begin to make amends.

I Remember You

I remember when
you cut up clothes to make an outfit for Pooh Bear,
and it was actually good,
and you could build anything from a spare,
leftover piece of wood.

I remember when
you made a 3-D city out of paper
because you were grounded from your toys,
and then went on to your next caper
without making any noise.

I remember when
you wrote poems in a notebook and read them to me
with pride.
You were sensitive and creative.
For Halloween you dressed like a bride,
making a costume or a craft, always so inventive.

I remember
you directing plays in the backyard.
You'd organize the neighbors and give them all a part.
A natural leader, their complaints you'd disregard.
You never let anyone deter you from your art.

I remember
you were best friends with your brother,
but you still needed time alone.

You never needed others,
but your love was always known.

I remember
Chinese food on a blanket on the floor,
watching movies and laughing till it hurt,
TV marathons, *Charmed* and *Veronica Mars* before
ice cream for dessert.

I remember
camping and hiking through the woods
and playing board games as it rained.
Safe inside the camper, we both understood
in this tiny space, so much love's contained.

I remember
caramel apples in autumn
and pumpkin-picking in the patch,
decorating the balsam
with favorite ornaments on each branch.

I remember
costumes and trick-or-treating in the snow,
sipping cocoa and baking cookies while
Frosty, the Snowman and every classic show
played on TV; it still makes me smile.

I remember
painting together and making crafts,
Old Colorado City at Christmas time,
snapping selfie photographs,
and holiday traditions I'll never leave behind.

I remember
hiking in the Garden of the Gods,
then talking round and round,
hanging out just because
as friends, we were bound.

I remember
decorating for every time of year,
roasting marshmallows in the fireplace;
it's a tradition for us here;
such a coziness you've given to this place.

I remember when
we went and got tattoos
together one summer day
and meeting you at Montague's,
whiling the time away at our favorite café.

I remember when
I visited you at the fire station
and saw you in your gear.
You were such an inspiration,
brings to my eye a tear.

I remember when
you saved a baby's life one day.
My heart just filled with pride—
extraordinary, no matter what you say.
I know you can do whatever you decide.

I remember when
you grew into a woman, independent and strong.

I see you in your uniform, ready for the day,
knowing you were the hero all along,
a stethoscope around your neck, going on your way.

I remember
swelling up, seeing you standing there,
a small woman, a large black truck,
big dog next to you, going anywhere
you feel is next; seeing you I'm struck

because I remember
there's never been a time I was not proud of you.
I cherish the times that draw us nearer,
closer I grow to you.
I'll love you forever; I've never seen it clearer.

than when I remember you.

Old Dogs

Old dogs
Gray around the temples and chin
Walk with a limp
A stiff gait
But still try to chase squirrels up gnarled oaks
Old dogs
Still enjoy slow strolls down friendly streets
Sniffing everyone they meet
Greeting neighbors and young pups
Even though they don't smell much anymore
Old dogs
Reminisce about their youth
Days when you threw the ball in the park
And they could run like the wind and you tired long
before them
Old dogs
Are more interested in tummy rubs and loving scratches
behind the ears
Than in begging for treats
Or playing tug-of-war with an old rope
But they'll still gather the energy to play
If it will make you happy
Old dogs
Embarrass easily
When the mailman sneaks up on them unnoticed
They look around to make sure you didn't see them
Letting down their guard
Old dogs

Try hard to do their duties
Even if you tell them that it's time
Time for them to be cared for now
Old dogs
Will muster up excitement when you come in the door
After a long hard day
They won't let you think for a moment
That you weren't missed
Old dogs
Fall asleep next to you and don't wake up when you leave the room
When they do wake, they struggle to their feet
Joints stiff, and go searching for you
Old dogs
Are wiser than young dogs
They know the value of a life-long friendship
They don't care about slippers anymore
Just companionship and loyalty
Old dogs
Can't hear or see very well
Except with their hearts
They are selfless souls
Growing more pure with each passing year
Old dogs
Feel shame if they can't keep up with you
Until they see their own heart shining back at them
And then they know
They've taught you what you needed to learn
Their work is done
Because when old dogs
Take a piece of your heart
With them when they go

You're still better off for having known them
Because with an old dog
Your heart grows larger through each and every
Old dog you've ever loved.

Flood

Always raining, never stopping
Oh, so draining, constant sopping
Flooding, scrubbing
Scouring the stains
Pouring your rains
Drowning, drenching
Set me free; I'll never be
Pristine clean
But saturated, sodden
Sinking in your sea
The flood unending
I go on offending
You remain unbending
Floundering, doubting
You allowing
This, my flood
Staggering through the mud
Let me go
To reap what I sow

From Long Ago Dreams

When once I was lost among the screams
Thrusting through the unbroken succession
I recognized you from long ago dreams

Sinking and swimming up bubbling streams
Struggling against such dark oppression
When once I was lost among the screams

Terrifying images and nightmarish themes
Immersed in the sensory impression
I recognized you from long ago dreams

Demons boast of savage rapines
Resisting their pull of possession
When once I was lost among the screams

Overwhelmingly driven to rabid extremes
Turning, I stumble through the procession
When I recognized you from long ago dreams

Far and away, a glint of light gleams
Gasping for breath, I make my confession
That once I was lost among those screams
When I recognized you from long ago dreams

Country

Cascading watercolor gravel
Winds and descends
'round shady bends
Decaying pastel stones
Trip precariously over hills
The breeze
kisses the scented pines
Whispering clouds
Tell secrets
As the wind awakens
Russet leaves
Swoop and swirl in a mock tornado
While the maddening
Ticking
Of the insect population
fades to silence
A dazzling autumn
Day in the country
Peaceful
and
Chaotic

A Willow Bends

A willow bends to the wind.
In approbation, she attends,
pledging fealty to the goddess.
The goddess waxing great, her promise.
An accomplice, sacrosanct yet equal,
she presides. Congenial,
she pulls the tide.
Bursting wide,
streams spill,
worshipping still
with their liquid hands,
sculpting stones
and building thrones
and shaping earth,
growing shallow for rebirth.
Cracked and dried beauty,
the brittle earth, ripe to be
encompassed in fire.
The elements conspire,
bringing the seedling forth anew.
Draped in the morning dew,
the seedling willow weeps
in joy, breathing deep
the ether of the stars,
and growing aging scars,
the willow reaches to her goddess,
the promise of her solace.
Then slowly the willow bends
in acquiescence to the wind.

An Ocean of Possibility

Language in a thousand pieces
Inadequate to express
An ocean in a million directions
Overwhelmed but not afraid
The obvious creates meaning
Without limitations
Another recognizes the idea
As my mind reconsiders beauty
A jungle of first impressions
I dream of the possibility
I compose it
This silhouette
From my desires
The passion in me
Turns my reality into
Dreams

Nothing's Ever Been the Same

The sun shone brighter
When you were born
The world got lighter
The cold grew warm

Flowers bloomed larger
Joy was realized
You became a harbor
For hope idealized

You're uniquely independent
Curious and strong-willed
Resolutely ascendant
With dreams to fulfill

Somewhat of a loner
No one could tell you what to do
I've always known there
Was no stopping you

The world grew fuller
With you in it
Filled with color
And promise within it

Creative and artistic
And lovingly attentive
Empathetic, altruistic

Imaginatively inventive

Love unimagined
Began the day you came
Beauty happened
And nothing's ever been the same

A Voice Whispers

A voice whispers
A solution
The sound
Echoes
In this life
Echoes of thoughts
Of love
Of truth
Resounding and inspiring
Life
Starts over
Without fear
A perfect world
"Tomorrow,"
A voice whispers

Helpless Anger

Through the tempest,
We shake and shiver
Though the chaos, we apprenticed
Still, with anger, we quake and quiver
Rage within us swells
Helpless anger
Silenceth the warning knells
Bidding danger
Righteous wrath unfolding
All for naught
Justice, in vain, upholding
For in a trap, you're caught
Powerless in position
Lowered notably in estimation
Self-control, the great physician
A worthier, by far, destination

Questions

The soul clings to its impressions
A deeper seed it plants
There are no answers to my questions

Searching for release of its expressions
In adoration the soul will dance
As it clings to its impressions

Powerless and prone to take suggestions
Promised such beauty, it's entranced
Yet, there are no answers to my questions

Lost in amazement, the processions
Gather at the feet of Romance
The soul clings to its impressions

Diminishing material possessions
Quenching spring, the soul's desire, it grants
Still, there are no answers to my questions

No remedy for our transgressions
No vague emptiness, it supplants,
But the soul clings to its impressions,
And there are no answers to my questions.

Trust

If you were to lie to me, I'd be forever lost
Wandering through the darkness of the trees
Among the cold and lonely frost

Clinging to the confidence, no matter what the cost
There's a scent of hope in the breeze,
But if you were to lie to me, I'd be forever lost

In the icy wind, tossed
Deserted, no one to hear my pleas
Among the cold and lonely frost

Ignoring the voice inside, fear glossed
Believing by degrees,
But if you were to lie to me, I'd be forever lost

Between barricades I'd never attempt to cross,
Trapped in a prison of dying leaves,
Swirling among the cold and lonely frost

But seeing into you, trust embossed,
My nervous heart is eased,
But if you were to lie to me, I'd be forever lost
Among the cold and lonely frost

Entropy

Shimmering snow, delicate and fine
Each intricate flake is one
Unique in its design
But just another drop of water in the burning sun

Forming into crystals
Its hardening has begun
Then melting, drips—it ripples
Just another drop of water in the burning sun

Flakes, so fragile
Their formations, valiantly they've won
Glittering, they dazzle
But last but a moment in the burning sun

Smoothly frozen once again
Now merging into one
Newly impenetrable until when
It's just another drop of water in the burning sun

Change is constant, it is written
Transformation is never done
The end is always hidden
In a drop of water in the burning sun

When at last, a vapor, it surely will succumb
To the scorching of the burning sun

A Caress from the Wind on the Sea

A caress from the wind on the sea
Gentle and warm on a sandy shore
Softly, it sweeps across me
Drawing me deeper, it's more
Than I imagine I need
This caress from the wind on the sea

Lightly,
Sand peppers my skin
Its synchronicity
Exists in the whim
The air surrounding me
A caress from the wind on the sea

Awakening,
To its embrace
The scent of salt lingering
Leaving its gentle trace
Breathing life into me
My caress from the wind on the sea

Languorously,
Dreaming on a sandy shore
The wind stirring attentively
I would not ask for more
When you come to me
A caress from the wind on the sea

Endless Night

Oh come, Sweet Golden Days;
Your fruitful deeds I long to praise.[1]
Cast away the hideous night.
Bring the birth of simple light.[2]
With heavy fear I grow weary,
Passing away nights so dreary.
Endless nights of insomnia
Bring to me a longing of
Idle days of warm surrender,
Lazy naps in grassy splendor,
Where demons of dark disappear
And light destroys shadowy fear.
I long for dawn's glorious light
When night's demons are out of sight.
Though I wish, I can't make the sun,[3]
Nor my desire make it come.
And daylight refuses to shine,
And I won't sleep till it is mine.
How long am I denied the light?
Must I be doomed to walk the night,[4]
As a ghost unable to rest

---

[1] From John Milton's *Paradise Lost*, Book 5, and also Eph. 5:11: "Have nothing to do with the fruitless deeds of darkness."
[2] From "Fern Hill" by Dylan Thomas: "So it must have been after the birth of the simple light...," wherein Thomas is describing the beauty of daylight.
[3] From Andrew Marvell's "To His Coy Mistress:" "Thus, though we cannot make our sun/Stand still, yet we will make him run." Unlike the narrator in Marvell's poem, this narrator wishes to make the sun and make it stay, though he cannot.
[4] From Shakespeare's *Hamlet*, I.v.14: "Doom'd for a certain term to walk the night." Hamlet's father's ghost was doomed to walk the night until his death was avenged.

Wanders in limbo, awaiting his test?
What great sin have I committed
That to live in light's forfeited?
Gazing upon the nightly shore,
Why only this and nothing more?[5]
Arise, Sweet Light, and tell your story.
Fill the earth with your trailing glory.[6]
Illuminate the earth; erase
This dense mass of blackness I face.
Be still, Sun, like to a coy
Mistress.[7] My love may grow and joy
Of you shall never grow tired
Of that truth in your orange fired
Heat, beating down the fear unknown—
But always present till it's shown
In light of day, impotent
To change its importunate
Branch into an icy hand,
Reaching through death to the hand
Of its lost love.[8] But instead,
Saves this sorcery for dead
Of night, when the sun goes down
And it is cold.[9] I shiver 'round

---

[5] This phrase comes from Edgar Allen Poe's "The Raven:" "Ghastly grim and ancient raven wandering from the Nightly shore" refers to the shore where the raven lives. "Only this and nothing more" refers to the constant "tapping at his chamber door," while the speaker wishes for tomorrow to come.
[6] From H.G. Wells' *The Island of Doctor Moreau*. Wells describes daylight as "the trailing glory of the sun" when the horrible night is ended, and they are safe from the animal/human hybrids.
[7] From Andrew Marvell's "To His Coy Mistress." The speaker is telling his mistress that if there were enough time, he would take his time cultivating her love for him and never get tired of doing so.
[8] From Emily Bronte's *Wuthering Heights*. Mr. Lockwood reaches out his window to silence the "importunate branch," and instead, takes hold of the "icy hand" of the ghost of Catherine Linton looking for her love, Heathcliff.

The dim fire that can only cast
Light for a shadow, but not last
Through these dark hours where evil
Exalted[10] makes us believe all
Shadows hide something wicked
This way coming,[11] through a thicket;
Perhaps a Goblin selling fruit
From the unquenchable hunger root.[12]
Or maybe evil in disguise,
Waiting, ready to devise
Some trick, disguised as some dark
And terrible Hound. Its bark,
Low and growling with blazing
Eyes and dripping jaws,[13] gazing
Like elver-gleams[14] in the night.
No, no, not night it is, but death.[15]
I shut my eyes and hold my breath—
Waiting, waiting—like Errour's den.[16]
This is no place for living men.
Mortal, I dare to dream these dreams
Never dreamed before;[17] though it seems

---

[9] From Stevie Smith's "The New Age:" "The sun is going down and becoming cold." This refers to the ending of an age, and the beginning of a darker, more terrible age.
[10] From Sir Arthur Conan Doyle's *The Hound of the Baskervilles:* "Those dark hours where the powers of evil are exalted."
[11] Originally from Shakespeare's *Macbeth*, though I refer to the novel by Ray Bradbury, *Something Wicked This Way Comes.*
[12] From Christina Rosetti's "The Goblin Market," where a young girl is seduced by goblins to eat dangerously addictive fruit, resulting in death.
[13] From Sir Arthur Conan Doyle's *The Hound of the Baskervilles.*
[14] From Seamus Heaney's "Station Island:" "Elver-gleams in the dark of the whole sea." Elver-gleams refers to the bright shine of young eels in the dark.
[15] This is from W.B. Yeats' poem "Easter 1916:" "No, no, not night but death" refers to the dark times of war-torn Ireland.
[16] From Edmund Spenser's "The Faerie Queene," I.i.13.
[17] From Edgar Allen Poe's "The Raven:" "Dreaming dreams no mortals

It is not sleep from which they come,
But waking dreams of horror from
Half-imagined dark things[18] trading
Places in the shadow, waiting
To strike when finally I sleep.
There must be more than this. I creep
To confront my fears, face to face.
My tired mind plays tricks on me
Increasing fear of what I see.
Riddles in the dark[19] seem to ask
Who I am beneath my mask.
This night, the pestilence that stalks[20]
Me, drifts along beside me, walks
With me—drives me to an answer,
Fills me with dread, my soul's cancer,
To that overwhelming question[21]
That still plagues my meditation.
What terrible beauty is born[22]
In darkness that serves to warn
Us of the evil in our soul?
Is it wickedness that fills the hole?
Or does the darkness aim to deceive
The better part of what we believe?
Are we forced to stay in the cave, all

---

ever dared to dream before." This passage refers to the narrator staring into the darkness and having visions due to his fear.
[18] From J.R.R. Tolkien's *The Hobbit*. When Bilbo and the others are in the dark cave, they see "half-imagined dark things" because of the incredible blackness of the dark.
[19] This refers again to J.R.R. Tolkien's *The Hobbit*. While in the dark cave, they were given riddles to answer.
[20] From *The NIV Study Bible:* "Nor the pestilence that stalks in the darkness" in Psalms 91:6.
[21] From T.S. Eliot's *The Love Song of Alfred J. Prufrock*, in which the narrator is being led to some "overwhelming question" that he is dreading.
[22] From W.B. Yeats' "Easter 1916:" "All changed, changed utterly: A terrible beauty is born."

Watching images reflected on the wall?[23]
Never to know the daylight's grace;
Never to leave this darkened place.
What is it that makes me tremble?
What in darkness does preamble?
In the night, thoughts are mutable.
Like the wicked, I am culpable—
My way is like deep darkness,[24]
Dulling my mind's sharpness.
This eternal night holds the blame
For in sweet sunlight, I've no shame.
My soul's blackness filled with light
Erases shadows of the night,
And my heart's free to rise up like
The morning dove, and the lark
At dawn rising to see morning[25]
Come and to the sky adorning
With their beauty added to
Break of day's colorful hue.
But I'm alone with the silence[26]
Of the night, which is the essence
Of my soul's ill contemplation—
Endless night's consideration.
Time—time enough to remember,
To rehash and reconsider,
Time for regret and dismay.
The lengthy night lingers late

---

[23] From Plato's "Allegory of the Cave," wherein people stay down in a cave watching images reflected on the wall, instead of living a real life. They do not know they can come out and see the real world in daylight in the real sunshine, rather than the artificial light of the fire in the cave.
[24] Proverbs 4:19: "But the way of the wicked is like deep darkness, they do not know what makes them tremble."
[25] From Shakespeare's "Sonnet 29:" "Like to the lark at break of day arising..."
[26] From H.G. Wells' *The Island of Doctor Moreau:* "I was alone with the night and silence."

Enough to murder and create[27]
Myself a thousand times and more.
Oh, come Sweet Light, I beg you, please,
End this night, my thoughts to ease.
Flood the earth[28] with your rays of light;
Destroy the evil of the night.
I'm not righteous but in day.
Redeem me from my thoughts and stay
Close by me and help me cope.
Spread over me new hope.
Let not the brooding darkness spread
His jealous wings[29] o'er me, but dead,
Your lonely nightingale, instead.
Soar, Sweet Lark, above my head.
Reach Heaven's gate[30] and open wide
The floodgates of grace and the tide
Of forgiveness; let loose on me—
Lighten my soul. Forever be
My foot's lamp, a light for my path[31]—
Redemption from my soul's wrath.
Come, Precious Peace, dropping slow
From morning's veils[32] and sunlight's glow.
Warm my body and my soul;

---

[27] From T.S. Eliot's "The Love Song of Alfred J. Prufrock:" "There will be time/To prepare a face to meet the faces that you meet/There will be time to murder and create."
[28] Refers to the Great Flood, wherein God destroyed the earth with water because of the people's wanton evil in Genesis 6:13.
[29] From John Milton's "L'Allegro:" "Where brooding Darkness spreads his jealous wings,/ And the night-raven sings." This is the poem that this poem is emulating, regarding the supremacy of the day over night.
[30] Again, this refers to Shakespeare's "Sonnet 29:" "Like to the lark at break of day arising/From sullen earth sings hymns at heaven's gate."
[31] From Psalm 119:105: "Thy Word is a lamp unto my feet and a light unto my path."
[32] From W.B. Yeats' "The Lake Isle of Innisfree:" "for peace comes dropping slow,/Dropping from the veils of the morning to where the cricket sings."

Spread me out on a grassy knoll.
To peaceful slumber, I will fall
Till the evening comes to call.
Then I'll rage against the dying[33]
Light and I will go on trying,
Though the dark leads the dimming bright
Gently into that evil night.

---

[33] From Dylan Thomas' "Do Not Go Gentle Into That Good Night:" "Do not go gentle into that good night./Rage, rage against the dying of the light."

Music

Music wraps his arms around me
And tells me he knows what I'm about
He shows me I'm not alone and speaks to me
In ways you couldn't even shout

He squeals and strums and screams to me
And then quietly whispers he accepts
All that you could never see in me
And all that you reject.

No one can destroy you like a child

Born out of your flesh, birth of the sacred
Adored
Loved unconditionally, while
You stand spurned, shorn
Of all aspect of affection
Unjust deflection, dejection unending
Saturated, consumed, unbending
Rending nights of mourning
Hours of scorning
Heights of sorrow, teetering
On a glimmer of tomorrow
Tears adorning the lifeless
The helpless, bought and owned
By your own blood
How else could
You be destroyed by a child?
No one else can slice you in half
With a word or a smile, put you on trial
For trying
What's left of you dying
Doomed to go on amending
Defending the right to hope
A press to tamp down the hurting
Until you're cut fresh
Veins spurting, you lay broken
Crumpled in a heap, racked with grief
Burning hollows weep
No relief, no light

Appears, calling me to go
Forced to remain, it's worse
Worse than you ever feared
Because who knew?
The pain you accrue
The depth of the blow
It's an effort to stand and smile
When you've been destroyed by a child.

Signs of Life

Shuffling through the gray
Blind to each delicate breath
These intricacies hold no sway
Cheerfully uttered throughout the day
The meaningless pleasantries
Each effort you weigh
The cost of transparency
With each sigh, a bray
You wake and remember what's lost
Momentarily defray
Smothered in civility
Fashioning smiles of clay
Blinking back signs of life
You purpose to allay
The squall of consciousness
Then take a breath and fly away

Waiting for the Light

They say weeping is only for the night
And joy comes in the morning
But we're still waiting for the light

History is hope's blight
Recorded as a warning
Yet weeping is only for the night

Wiping out evil, He will smite
Rid the world of its scorning
But we're still waiting for the light

Will we be next on this holy height,
Self-righteousness adorning?
Will our weeping be only for the night?

As dark clouds swarm and reunite
We brace against His storming
Pointlessly waiting for the light

With words we find so trite
But will never end our mourning,
Yet weeping is only for the night
So we go on waiting for the light

Rebellious by Nature

Rebellious by nature
I resist the pull
The Knowing
A pushing back against the wind
The ache I'm sure will dull
Rebellious by nature
I flee from Your hand
You don't make sense to me,
Yet I may believe
Putting on my mask of incredulity,
I rationalize, legitimize the reasons I can't know
But Your face is all I see
Every song I hear, every stab I feel
Every whisper in my ear
A reason for the chaos
The reason I'm a wreck
The sinking in my stomach,
The stone of dread around my neck
Rebellious by nature
Pride and shame mix inexplicably
Kindness and compassion, love and harmony
How can it be that that's not good enough?
What's wrong with me?
Obedience, submission—words of contempt
Drawn into adoration, I don't want to admit
Useless, the attempt
Impossible, unreasonable
Incomprehensible
Let me be
Rebellious by nature

Married to You

Sun splashes across our bed.
We wake, slowly unwrapping our tangled selves,
Shifting, intertwining again in a different position.
Your eyes gradually open; the bluest eyes I've ever seen.
Your slow smile warms me, and I smile in return.
This is what it's like to wake up with you.

At work, you leisurely stroll through my mind a thousand times.
You're my favorite daydream.
My key turns in the lock after a busy day.
The smell of coffee and the music of your guitar
Greet me at the door.
This is what it's like to come home to you.

You make a silly face, pull your pants up to your chest
Just to make me laugh.
Laughter and love always fill our home.
It feels like peace in your arms.
This is what it's like to be home with you.

Honesty fills our home,
Acceptance is our style.
Being with you is serenity
Joy in who we are
Individually and together
Being ourselves in complete tranquility.
This is what it's like to be married to you.

The Sun Still Rises

The sun still rises in the morning; the moon still shines at night.
Somehow we see a future, and imagine it will stay,
But the wind still blows in Eden, despite the wrong and right.

Trying to determine when to run and when to fight,
We muster up the courage, but will the cost outweigh?
The sun still rises in the morning; the moon still shines at night.

Change is in the atmosphere, whether or not it's right.
The forecast calls for stillness, yet we know they
Believe the wind still blows in Eden, despite the wrong and right.

We gather up our forces; we fight with all our might
Just to see our soldiers crumble, lost to another fray,
But the sun still rises in the morning; the moon still shines at night.

Rising up once more, we stumble, grasping at the light.
Squinting through the brightness, we take a breath and pray
That the wind still blows in Eden, despite the wrong and right.

Someday we'll see a future: oh, it's a perfect sight,

And we will hold it in our hearts and imagine it can stay,
For the sun still rises in the morning; the moon still shines at night.
And the wind still blows in Eden, despite the wrong and right.

In Memorium

Artistically, you painted the world
Acquainted with beauty
You saw it that way
Depicting the everyday
Uniquely honest
Each delicate stroke promised
An interpretation of the significant
A quiet determination for creative expression
With wisdom, you directed
A symphony of family
But individually affected
Orchestrating warmth and growing commitment
Each gathering, its essence, contentment
Every holiday glowing
With tradition and meaning
Each addition warmly welcomed
The whole place teeming
In laughter and joy
Preparing a feast
Your generosity without cease
Your grace given spontaneously
And in humor you viewed
A world of contradictions
Firmly imbued your convictions
Making sense of the chaos
Even the loss
Seeing through to the importance
Of sharing a life, moments rife

With significance
Independent you persisted, making do
With simple things existence brings
Fashioning something wonderful
Out of necessity, a recipe for happiness
With a strength innate
Holding your ground, fiery and fierce
Loyally bound
Your influence on us permanently embossed
Each of us pierced
With the pain of your loss

I Know

Please don't tell me
what I already know,
what I don't believe
anyway
'cuz I've considered the source,
so where are these angels
sent to deliver us?
Heard it before, no need to discuss

I know, I know

God's not a vending machine
but I'm not asking for a Coke
I've heard the clichés
I'm not buying today
Mom's dying and Dad's in jail
Sister's going to foster care
and I'm going to hell

I know, I know

His ways are not ours
How could we expect them to make sense?
He never gave you a mind 'cuz you was supposed
to think
Shut it up tight and believe with all your might
One might think he really doesn't want you to believe
Don't listen to reason; it's just there to deceive

I know, I know

He's our invisible friend
in the sky
We need to have faith,
faith like a child
because only a child could believe it
Santa Claus and the Easter Bunny's
our path to perceive it

I know, I know

God is good no matter what he does
He always gets a pass
Find a parking space—Praise God
No answer to prayer? He's just telling you to wait
I lose my job? He has a plan,
no worries; it's better than Crack,
hardly any withdrawal when you come off this Smack

I know, I know

He works in mysterious ways
and it's not his fault, 10,000 die in an earthquake
or six million Jews at the hand of his creation
We just live in a broken world
because some chick had no willpower
Of course, who are we to question that logic?
If you do, he may well devour
you in that last hour.

I know, I know

It'll be okay, some day, some day
in eternity,
the imaginary place where God makes up for all the shit
he did to you in this life,
your only life
Don't hold your breath
Go ahead and breathe while you can
There ain't gonna be no TV angels
coming to touch your miserable life
Maybe, if you're lucky,
he'll just ask you to sacrifice your child
to prove your loyalty

I know, I know

At the last minute he yells, "Psych!"
All in good fun,
after all, he murdered his son
See what a good father does?
He'll cure your cancer—don't call it remission
even though it will probably come back
but don't ask him to grow back limbs
'cuz he's a union fan
Do you really want to spend eternity
with this man?
That's blasphemy,
I know,
a travesty because we only exist to glorify this
That's morality?
I don't think so.
I know what I know.

Music Lives Here

A special kind of music lives here
Amidst the mountain mist
Its benevolence is strangely clear
The circling of a breeze so crisp
Carries its message softly to my ear
The oneness of the universe insists
On fracturing my frail veneer
Lost in this musical tryst
A twig breaks—a deer
Meeting, our gaze lingers—we coexist
In this moment, we disappear
Through millennia, we drift
Lifted beyond the stratosphere
Soaring above the swift
Spirits who insouciantly appear
Dipping down into the midst
Of crested mountains sheer
Eagles, we enlist
To retrieve a souvenir
Of this infinite moment where we exist
When the music living here
Brushed us with its fragrant kiss
And disappeared

Reversal

Gazing thickly through the mist
Vagaries fade into the impassable
Tracing ambiguous signs, I persist
In foolishly pursuing the intangible

Finally awake, I see the irrational—
The loss of something that doesn't exist
Arming myself, I'm intractable
I ready myself to resist

Oddly, I mourn the infallible
A loving mirage is dismissed
Reality is not compatible
With the spikes in your wrist

Light exposes the actual
Meaning of which it consists
Accepting that which is substantial
Disillusioned, I desist

Following the path of the rational
Another paradigm shift
Reversal, a practical
Undertaking adrift

Hanging on to the palpable
The evidence I enlist
Stoically casual
I betray this fantasy with a kiss

Those Eyes

She loved me with those eyes
Large and brown, staring up at me
The wisdom of the ages implied

Whether to apologize
Or merely out of curiosity
It was always with love in those eyes

Her soft gaze intensified
Watching over me carefully
The wisdom of the ages implied

Always she sympathized
Laying her head on my knee
Loving me with those eyes

Patiently she sighed
Waiting on me dutifully
The wisdom of the ages implied

Short are the days love multiplies
She spent them on loyalty, joyfully
Loving me with those eyes
The wisdom of the ages implied

Tossed

On a blue-green marble,
I wander without knowing
A fervent explorer
Observing this
And wondering about that
What is truth?
I'm a paper caught by the wind
Struggling to put my feet on the ground
To give chase
Rolling and tumbling 'round each bend
Farther away, always
An inch or two out of reach
Always the truth
Tossed high by the wind
Of this conviction or that
I miss the meaning of here
Dipping low across
A viridian blue sphere
I never quite land
Before the need again
Rises up in me
Flinging me across
An alabaster sea
A desert of need that
Predates me
Just a spot on a blue-green marble

Black and White Promises

Dusty on the mantle
Framed in delicate design
Opening, I dismantle
Faces lost in time
Black and white promises
Of seeing you again
Begin again the processes
Of grieving you and then
I hold your image close to me
And think of how you were
Strong arms that held me tenderly
And told me you were sure
That I'd grow up to be someone
Of whom you'd be so proud,
But Daddy, you're not the only one
Whose heart is swollen now
Gazing at your picture
Solemn young men dressed
To bravely face the future
In their Sunday best
My father and his brother—
Two boys on leave from war
A future to uncover
I couldn't ask for more
Your life continues to inspire
Your wisdom I replay
A father to learn from and admire
And I miss you every day.

Art

A canvas
Colors vividly swirl
A painted sky
Cloud-swept and clean
A sharp and jagged mountain
Cut with a palette knife
The paint tells a story of its own
Not realistic but real
More real than nature
The truth underneath
Revealing
What the soul sees
What the heart knows
Life uncovered
Art shows the true story
A story so important
Not everyone can understand it
The unfortunate go blindly
Through mountains and meadows
By seascapes and down winding paths
Looking but never seeing
While the artist strips away the veil
And brightens the picture
Revealing what was there all along
Hidden from the ordinary
Knowing there is no such thing
The extraordinary is all around us
Hiding, pretending to be banal, bourgeois
Until the artist brushes truth
On a canvas

Done

Don't preach; I have believed
To live the life, I have aspired
But I am done being naïve

Once, I mistakenly perceived
And followed like a child
So don't preach; I have believed

Hope and fantasy interweaved,
Conditioned and beguiled
But I am done being naïve

Indoctrinated and deceived,
I sought to be reconciled
So don't preach; I have believed

Finally waking, the truth I have conceived
I'm not a sheep, nor am I a child
I am done being naïve

In truth, I am relieved
Though now I am reviled
So don't preach; I have believed
And I am done being naïve

Breathe

Just breathe
Sinking deeper, I turn inward
Searching for me
Just rest here awhile
Letting the thoughts drift
Along the outer edges of my mind
Immersed in my inner sanctuary
I don't need anything
Safe and alone
Peace settles over me like a soft blanket
Drift
Just breathe
The air filling my lungs
Satisfies me
I am content with nothing more than breath
Assuaged and serene
I rest
No expectations
With every exhalation
Taking me down
Further into me
A soft breeze kisses my skin
The wings of a bird flutter overhead
In a nearby tree
These images drift slowly in my mind
Before dissipating like fog in the sun
Just breathe

Tomb

Do you mean to kill me slowly?
Breath by breath
Smothering me with every withheld word
Every silent occasion
Your absence screams
What you won't say
Do you want to break me,
Utterly destroy me?
Do you even realize
Your words unspoken
Choked down and swallowed
Suck the air from the world?
Suffocating, desperate for relief
Sliding, grasping at anything
To assuage the pain that unexpectedly leaps
Into my consciousness
Pain that lies dull and dormant
Until the stillness arrives
Do you want to empty me?
Hollow me
Till I blow away in the wind?
Or turn me to vacant stone?
My slow transformation
Unexplained
In the darkness, I will the coldness to take over
Till I'm the tomb and not the body

Honesty

Like through crystal clear glass
I see you beyond
The unconscious impasse
Your words and your actions correspond

Not even a mist fogs this air
Things we share impossibly
Risking all that we care
For honesty

Because without it, we're just strangers
Alone in the world of the mind
Lonely traitors
Intimacy left behind

Without truth
We can't find each other
Play the game of sleuth
Why bother?

The real me misconstrued
The real you
Subdued
Living lives we never knew

So, with you, only honesty
I won't conceal me
No pretense; an improbability

But there's no lying harmlessly

No caravan of tales
I don't want to live alone
Because honestly, pretending pales
In the light of being known

Alone, I Thrive

Once again I'm drowning
With You nowhere to be seen.
Can't You see I'm floundering
In the open sea?

In my doubt I'm sinking,
Not knowing if You'll come.
I just can't help but thinking
More faith would help me some.

Could it be Your purpose
To let me drown again?
I think You are not merciless;
There must be a higher end.

I reach out to You, Oh Lord,
Grasping at Your hand.
I can see the distant shore,
The fabled Promised Land.

I feel Your hand is slipping.
There's nothing I can do.
I feel my heart is ripping,
But Your plan was all You knew.

Gazing at the inky sky,
I see the moonlight shine.
I tell myself I shouldn't cry

For Your will be done, not mine.

I tell myself, someday, You will let me see
The purpose in Your plan,
And I'll understand why You let me
Sink, slipping from Your hand.

I'll understand Your absence.
In time I'll comprehend
Why You don't come to my defense;
No doubt your reason will transcend.

The silence from You is deafening,
Abandoned once again.
My hope in You is lessening;
My withdrawal from You begins.

I don't blame You for Your failure to assist
Me; You are unable to respond.
You simply don't exist;
I should have known it all along,
But the idea—impossible to resist.

So alone in the water, I struggle to survive,
Rising to the surface, surging
Forward, I arrive.
To the shore emerging,
In tact, alone, I thrive.

Autumn

Nature's one demand is change.
Our years like seasons we cannot hold,
For Fates align and rearrange.

From green to gold and red, the range
Features a wondrous story told
Of Nature's one demand of change.

A painted impression from the artistic Mage,
A fractal of the life we hold
While Fates align and rearrange.

Beautiful dying, lovely and strange,
The agéd Wisdom, mysteries unfold,
For Nature's one demand is change.

In leafless branches, we seek a sage
To nurture and guide us into our gold
As Fates align and rearrange.

Measuring our days, we alone gauge
Our years like seasons, a sweet story told
Of Nature's only demand of change
As Fates align and rearrange.

Fickle

I've heard the shaming speech,
"She's fickle"
because I am ever learning,
reading books and reaching.
Thinking incessantly, they teach me.
I talk it out with others,
explorers discovering
ideas, vast and illuminating,
amassed in dusty volumes innumerable;
the spectres of a thousand dead thinkers,
they linger; searchers speak.
They are my kin.
I listen, the voices in them swirling.
I examine each to each, intuit
every chasmic breach.
Still I'm open to believing,
receiving their insight.
Perception is just a glimmer
in the blackness of the sky.
It remembers the light
a million light years away.
Does that make me fickle?
Easily led astray?
No, I am not gullible
but logical, rational in the extreme.
Reasoning through the proofs,
Evidence supreme while Wonder plays her part,
mysterious and elusive,

deleterious to the unknown
as the wisdom of the ancients
mingles in the understanding of the present,
a common endeavor—truth.
So, I may reconsider;
I guess I am fickle,
or should I shut my mind up tight?
Refuse to see the light?
Hang on to a fantasy
and close my eyes after glimpsing reality?
Unswerving and blind,
comfortably stable?
No, I'll be fickle,
reliably capricious,
always acknowledging
for some, life is a path toward enlightenment,
a journey that has no clear destination,
no deterministic end,
a winding path, a road with a bend,
even a switchback or two,
just a rest stop here and there,
a place to catch your breath,
to be aware
that knowledge is an adventure,
spreading out before me,
a road measured in years rather than miles,
and wisdom is a temporary state of mind.
I won't be shamed for being fickle.
My mind is mine to change,
and the path I choose so fine.

I Grieve

Lost and faltering
Floundering in the sea
Of my indispensable need
Need that intensifies in the darkness
Unlimited and unending
How can I describe
The hollowness of loss?
Do I speak?
Will I risk the words
That once released continue
Out of control throughout the breath of eternity?
Shall I know the result
Of these intemperate thoughts?
Or slumber in the oblivion of the dead?
O, tranquil are the deaf
To the choruses of loss
For to speak, to give voice
To that which is in reality
A scream
Would spin this wheel interminably,
Or if it be little more than a squeak
Choked and muffled by grief,
Stutter and trip
to a premature conclusion
How then do I proceed
When lost and faltering, I grieve?

Masterpiece

I paint a masterpiece
My soul, a brush
Loving colors
Brilliant with love
A glorious metaphor
You appear surreal
A shimmering impression
A vibrant smattering
All of you a landscape
Free
Alive and individual
My love, a palette
To paint the beauty
Of my emotion
My impression
You
a masterpiece

Bareback in the Meadow

Softly in the meadow, brushing back his mane,
Bareback rider, farm girl among the golden grain
Growing in her faith, overcome with dreams,
A vision of a life, within her eye it gleams.

She swears her vows one cold December day,
Knowing there'll be struggles that will come their way.
With only hope and true love to keep her warm,
With strength and poise, she faces every storm.

Raising up a family, five to call her own,
Colorful blocks of fabric, lovingly she's sewn,
A close-knit mosaic, a family replete,
Heirloom of a mother, a priceless quilt complete.

Ever she is working, sacrificing to provide.
Surrounded by her progeny, life is simplified.
Always she is faithful and takes the time to pray
For cares to be forgotten and blessings for the day.

When days are long, but time grows short
Together they support; they quietly exhort
A heritage of devotion she continues to convey,
Her lasting legacy, a magnificent array.

She says farewell to her love until they meet again,

Until that day that she will go and meet her love and when
She'll live forever with her Lord and pain will go its way,
No worries to escape and all burdens fly away.

She struggles through the seasons without him at her side,
And when it's time to join him, all before is justified.
She leaves her clan with memories of her tender heart,
Tears she shed in worry, prayers said when they're apart.

And many more of joyful days, her love they testify
Of birthday get-togethers and stories of days gone by,
Christmas mornings filled with love, baking just for fun,
And homemade ice cream on the porch in the summer sun.

So, she says farewell to her loves until they meet again,
Waiting for the reunion, when she will be with them.
She spends her days with her groom and her Lord by her side,
And softly in a meadow, her dreams are realized.
Among the golden grain, they ride side by side,
Bareback in the meadow and across the countryside.

Safe

When I stare point-blank
Into all that is not there
And realize this sham
For what it is, the mist
Dries up; the fog dissipates like on the lenses of glasses
Unexpectedly, everything is clear
What, then, do I attribute
This unrelenting life?
How does one risk all
For one last roll of the dice
When the odds are always against?
Easy, easier still with nothing
Nothing left to grasp
Holding loosely, how can I not fall?
I see me slipping through cracks
I pretended not to see
Too dangerous, precarious at best
So, I am frozen to this unlikely spot
Reduced and fading as a dream
Uncharacteristically still
Furiously safe
Counting out my days like pennies in a jar
Abundant and worthless
Cruel irony that I know how to live
And yet
Refuse

I Dreamed of You Again Last Night

I dreamed of you again last night
As always, I searched for you despite
The distracting crowd of others gone
Desperate for just a glimpse in the throng
Above the heart-crushing mob
My hollowness behind a façade
Of going about my ordinary life
But my longing remains a knife
I hide behind all the day
But when the light gives way to gray
I submerge in the slumbering hope
In my subconscious relief, grope
Wondering why, always why
Do you know I cry
Every night whether I see you
Fall in your arms, and believe you
When you say you still love me
Or times when you are no where I see
When I wake, my face wet
With tears, unable to forget?
I'm starting to think I never will
The silence from you still
Batters me in the truthful dark
My memory of you leaves a mark
Do you ever dream of me, I wonder
When we meet in our slumber?
Are you really there somehow?
Or do I cross your mind at all now?

Sometimes your face interrupts the dawn
Just a glimpse and then you're gone
I know it's me who hides you in the light
But I'll search for you in my dreams tonight.

Free (#2, Letting Go)

Letting go
I let myself be who I am
Wandering alone through a jungle
Of contradictory claims
The skeptic
Ye of little faith
Actually none
Bouncing from one fiction to another
Grasping at scrawny tree limbs
Too dry and brittle to hold the weight of inspection
Of critical scrutiny
I hung on too long
Even while twigs snapped at a touch
Letting go
I should have done it long ago
Free-falling, uninjured
Floating peacefully on the unknown
It's never too soon to be free
At last, free to live
The reality, a genuine life
On the undiscovered details
Letting go
Of the need to know
Content
Free from the fairy tale
The false hope
Hope that meant nothing
More than an interesting dream

An afternoon of storytelling
An evening of Shakespeare
Both tragic and comedic
An epic battle between good and evil
Only to realize there is no difference
According to this dramatist
Letting go
And realizing the freedom
The relief
The ability to breathe deeply
Of the infinite, if only for a moment
A blip on the radar of the universe
A breath so pure and clean
I'd never miss the toxic perfume of lies
So I exhale completely
Letting go

Peaceful Harbor

Through the briny deep, a charter
Struggles in the swell
Until it finds a peaceful harbor

The unbounded crest beats harder
In the distance rings a knell
Through the briny deep, a charter

A cargo of hopes to martyr
In the distance, a chance to quell
For it will find a peaceful harbor

Drifting farther
To a tranquil berth to dwell
Through the briny deep, a charter

With the Fates, will hope to barter
A ponderous destiny to compel
It to that sweet and peaceful harbor

Forecasts presume gales much larger
But Fortune's will is to propel
It through the briny deep, a charter
Until it finds its peaceful harbor

Apprentice

Chipped wood
Nicked and dented
Purposely abused to create
What was not earned
Am I a craftsman then?
Or a liar?
Fabricated walls
"Aged" plaster
Crackled paint chips
Shards that flake off into
My shaking hand
Like broken glass
Glass like metal shavings
Their fragmented images
Steal my light
Sending it in a dozen different
Directions
Confusing me
With ambiguous fingers
Pointing first this way
Then that, iridescent swirling hope
A spectrum of half-truths
Promise the possibility
Of a lovely destruction
Even an apprentice can make something
Beautiful
Now and then

Book Tribe

A collective of common interests
An intellectual pursuit
Brought together by the simplest
A shared attribute
But in our group we found
A complex amity
The thread by which we're bound
Is not the latest read
An unexpected mingling
A mélange of fine wines
In laughter with glasses clinking
A friendship is forged over time
A kaleidoscope of voices
Diverse personalities
Apparent in our choices
Or when one disagrees
These differences don't chill
Our friendship
The warmth we feel is real
The kinship
The bond of our group
Is refreshingly compassionate
For such a varied troupe
Drama-free protagonists
Because conflict is no good
Encouragement is our shibboleth
Our alliance understood
We destroy the myth

Trust is our apothegm
We'd rather spend our time
On worthier whims
Or expanding of the mind
Whether interpreting the written word
Or sunning by the pool
Companionship is served
Gathered by the Yule
In winter or mineral springs in fall
On a weekend trip to the cabin
Or a movie at the mall
Whatever may happen
Whatever fate may decide
I'm glad I have this motley crew I affectionately call my tribe

Stop the World

You still my world and stop the turn
Of this manic swirl
Mesmerized and taciturn
Rescued from the tilt and whirl
The distractions of a life filled
To excess with nothingness
All at once is stilled
A quiet catalyst to reassess
The curious calm of standing still
You still my world and stop the turn
A gentle discovery of a pearl
Reflectively, I adjourn
From the spinning of the world

Remembering

I heard a melody so sweet
Sweet as the words you once whispered to me
A fragrant sound
A tender and unexpected chord
That at once lifts my soul
And tears my heart
A tinge of melancholy among the smiles
Suddenly invades me
Measure by measure
A symphony of memories
My whole being recalls you
Not a particular day
A certain event
But the entirety of you
Inseparable, the parts
Existing in a timeless encapsulation
Of every sweet experience
And simultaneously
The deep hollowness
The absence of you

Transformed

Sleeping through the everyday
Unconsciously conformed
Never noticing my malaise
When brewing there a storm
Dark skies block the rays
Clouds twist and deform
It's hard to find my way
Asleep, but in the form
Pain penetrates the gray
In loss I am reformed
In presence I appraise
The life I've lived and ways
Ways, my anguish informs
And in the balance weighs
Surviving pain transforms
Illuminated, consciously ablaze
Awake and knowing I will mourn
But joy I hold in yesterday
And love today is warm

Escape

Every day I escape
A retreat into my perfect place
Where moonbeams reflect off silver streams
And rainbow-colored butterflies
Dance on thin legs
On the tips of delicate veiny leaves
Sprouting from ancient gnarled oaks
A place where every loved one who has passed
Gathers to enjoy
The collective wisdom of a million lives
The adventures of *one* life combined
They speak to me in quiet love
In a single language, we each understand
The music of the breeze
And the rubbing of a cricket's feet
Older than time remembered
The only tears are those of joy
An epiphany so splendid
And pain, a distant memory
Is understood in gratitude
Each moment every day
All is still and time does not exist
My Eden is always here
Inside of me
A sweet serenity
My real self lives here
I visit her every day
No travel plans or bag to pack

In the plush warm grass under a sunshine sky
Or in the cozy haven of my home
All I have to do is sit
I close my eyes and drift
And every day I journey
To my perfect place—My lovely escape

The Stone

On the hillside hidden
Among the knotty pine
Lies a weathered stone of red
Sharp edges softened over time
Still the weight of it remains
Its sturdy strength sublime
A signpost to find your way
A monument, a shrine
Its presence is a constant
When confused among the pine
Kindly, it waits to comfort
And listen for a time
To any who lose their way
To rest and realign
It suffered every storm
And every passerby
Patiently awaiting
The elements to redefine
Its next stage of existence
Smoothed and refined
And finally dissolve it home again
Sinking ever to recline

The Broken Become Wise

Images of the long forgotten
Dance across closed eyes
A smoldering cauldron of misbegotten
Tries; faltering, I surmise
Too late the uncommon
Value of dark and stormy skies
The knowledge of the sodden
Soul; the broken become wise

Straining, I see through the mist of fear
The wisdom of the ancient Druid
Seer; her smile is cavalier
My dread is transmuted
Bravely, I appear
Sorrow, as a weed uprooted
Destiny—no mere
List, so easily permuted

I, alone, discern
The path of the Ancients
The Celtic sojourn learn
Deafened to mendacious
Guides, I finally adjourn
Rumination's patience
Prophetic dreams return
Asleep, the mind sagacious

Awakened, my pilgrimage is clear

Avoiding the spiritually reputed
Secluded, I pioneer
The skeptic, conduits refuted
Divining the allelic, finally truth is near
Facts undisputed
Though the Romantic's quest's sincere
Morosely, true believers brooded

Still, images of the long forgotten rise
But the broken become wise
And healed, the myth decries

Teacher

There's nothing quite like the light in the eyes of a student
Understanding dawning unexpectedly
A signpost discovered on a destined journey
Previously lost, the way revealed
Better still, enthusiasm kindled
The desire to know just for the sake of knowing
I can see it when our eyes meet
Suddenly and unanticipated
A kindred spirit
I see the spark glimmer
Sharing the love of a favorite poem
An incredible novel, words that move and stir
Words that burn and change them
The philosophical depth of Thoreau
The insight of Dickens
The straightforward profundity of Steinbeck
And then . . .
The birth of something new
The product of a student's pen
The baring of a soul, the beginning of knowing
Who they are and what they have to say
To a world listening, eager for a relationship
Between writer and reader, poet and philosopher
There's nothing better
A new writer, excitedly asking you to read his work
The pride in his eyes as you express your awe
In the phrases he creates

A new Whitman is born
And I contributed a verse
To the inspiration of a new generation
The state can't document this on a form
But I know what I've done
Evaluate away
I'll be right here, creating the Emersons of the future
My job is to find the spark in a student's eye
And ignite the fire.

Snow Day

An unexpected gift
Like waking up on Christmas morning
Brightly colored packages piled high by the tree
Sitting in the dim glow of the TV
The "Closed" message trails across the bottom of the screen
Outside, it's still dark but with a mysterious glow
Surreal, as if lit from some unknown source
The white sky, a snow globe, shaken
Oversized and intricately detailed flakes
Drift gently to the ground
Forming a lumbering blanket of white
Mounds drift and roll and disappear
Into the fog, the thick, wet air
Not quite frozen, heavy with the promise
Of more to come
I turn on the lights of the Christmas tree
The undulating glow casts a soft pattern on the wall
The village lights reflect on the glittery surface of the snow
My own private scene suspended in time
I light the fire and sit, absorbing the moment
The gift
A day to do anything, my own suspension of time
Life does not go on without me
I'm not missing anything
When I emerge from my snowy haven
Life will be just as I left it

Words Don't Fail Me

I dance this pen across the world
and all I am is set free.
Words become separate
lives unto themselves,
free to roam and do as they please,
to be sucked up by thirsty souls
and to be tossed aside as waste by others.
Sometimes ignored, unread
but still looming, like ghosts
invisible but present
or taken and changed—
Emerging,
interpreted and reinterpreted.
Unrecognizable to their maker,
they stretch and encircle.
Sufficient to their purpose,
words don't fail me.
Feelings impossible to quantify or understand
become tangible, ideas made substantial,
absorbed into the universe
yet marked as distinct.
Through words
I know and I am known.

Little Dog

Little dog
You're such a little human
You don't know who you're supposed to be
Where's my greeting at the door?
A lick on my palm, a wet kiss on my cheek?
Moody, you pout
When you feel a slight
Sensitive, you feel the right
To withhold your affection
Independent, you do what you want
You ignore me when I call
But when you feel like it, you come
And follow me around
I share everything I have
And you gladly accept
Then go about your business
As if you haven't got the time
To deal with my annoying pats
Didn't anyone ever tell you
you are a supposed to be a dog?
But then you confuse me
Wag your tail and give a woof
Obedient, you sit and wait patiently for a treat
And if kindness is a sign
Or gentleness the key
To a canine personality
Then you've mastered that most assuredly
The birds walk by you in peace and one accord

The squirrels dawdle lazily in your yard
Obviously in a relaxed state of mind
Even bugs crawl beneath your nose
Without the slightest sense of peril
Whatever complicated creature you are
Befuddling and bizarre, I'll take it
I'll give you my love and protection
And accept your moody sulking
And lack of affection, but just once in a while
Could you pretend to be just my little dog?

Bohemian Atheist

I've got my bellbottoms and tarot cards,
but I don't presuppose the divine;
dismissing science disregards
progress and favors magical design.
And though I prefer flowers over towers,
I draw the line at prayer.
Inaction really sours
compared to deeds anywhere.
Still, I enjoy a touch of Zen,
a little yoga under a leafy tree.
After all, there's a clear correlation,
de-stress and meditation;
it requires no special plea.
As for enjoying the vegetation,
a nature devotee,
the data's the confirmation
that this is a worthy state of mind.
I respect the earth,
to conservation I'm inclined;
preservation for future generation's birth,
and with all beings I'm entwined.
My survival's not unilateral,
as history substantiates,
nor dependent on the supernatural.
It's cooperation that necessitates.
And while I love the earth, I won't worship it.
I'd rather depend on rationalism.
I'm multifarious but not a hypocrite

even though my Buddha puts me in a peaceful state.
It's simply symbolism,
no higher self to elucidate.
Just this hippie chick
chillin' in my Existentialism,
no supernatural trick.
Crystals and full moons—
I don't dismiss them out of hand;
I won't necessarily impugn
these things we don't yet understand.
I'm open to the evidence,
but I won't believe just any tale.
There may be power in the elements,
but the scientific method I'll avail.
And I'll work for my fellow human,
fight injustice, and help the poor—
the humanistic acumen,
kindness the allure
because I'm an evolved member
of my hominid species.
My greed, I temper
with a social treaty
and a bit of liberalism,
rather than a divine delusion,
a healthy dose of skepticism.
I see through the illusion,
so while I may participate in protest
the notion's not the craziest.
My behavior manifests
in an anomaly, a Bohemian atheist.

Just Gone

I don't typically blame myself
For others' behavior
But I can't help but wonder why
One day you were just gone
I search the sinking pit inside
The place I feel your rejection most
But all I find is an empty hole
Left by you
Still I wonder—
Wonder why those I thought would never leave
Quietly disappear without a word
As if I wouldn't notice
I did
I look for you, reach out
But this is clearly no accident
No momentary lapse
You're gone, and you meant to be
Again, digressing into self-examination
Tearing at the seams of who I am
Searching through each word spoken
A useless pursuit
All I've done is be true
I've always been there for you
Treated you well
Never betrayed you

Unless, just being me is treachery
It's true, I think differently
I don't agree with your politics
Or your god
But it would be nice
If you remembered that I am more
Than those two things
I am more than your judgments
I am loyal and kind
Loving and generous
And accepting of you
Even though I disagree
I thought love was deeper than that
My mistake
I will take responsibility for expecting
More than you are capable of
But I won't blame myself for the loss of you
Because I would never have let you go
Never have let such little things come between us
I would never have just gone

All the Heaven and Hell

Lightly falling snowflakes
The loving eyes of my old dog
The smile of a baby
Red and gold leaves scattered on the ground
Glistening wet petals in the morning sun
This is all the heaven I will ever know

Holding the hand of my mother as she leaves me
Hot tears of loss, the indescribable pain in my chest
Holding my best friend as she takes her last breath
Angry words from a trusted mouth
Grave news from a doctor's chart
This is all the hell I will ever know

The soft glow of a crackling fire
Holding hands with the best man I've ever known
The swell of love his gaze makes me feel
The time spent with my closest friends
Laughing until my stomach hurts
This is all the heaven I will ever know

The anxiety of deadlines
The crushing weight of responsibilities
Debts to pay and artificial worries
The helplessness of age
The loneliness of loss
This is all the hell I will ever know

Pain and depression
Joy and the sweetness of love
Anger and frustration
Comfort and peace
Gratitude for all of this life
This is all the heaven and hell I will ever know

Lucky

Everything leads to tragedy
It seems to compound
But in the in-between
I am lucky
Fate smiles smugly
While I frown
But in the darkness, I am found
I am lucky
A little fussy
But I am bound
To this life
I am lucky
Heartfelt and enigmatic
I am rife
With friends all around me
I am lucky
In tenderness abounding
I swim through the sorrow
Willingly pursuing tomorrow
I am lucky
The knell has sounded
To set me free
But I ignore it, naturally
With troubles I am hounded
But I am lucky
In the midst of falling leaves
I am surrounded
An abundance of tears deceives

I'm inclined to opine
But still, I'm lucky
Flowers lose their petals
The foundation finally settles
But all around me I am grounded
In love, I'm astounded
And I'm so lucky
There's a chance to amend
Love enough to spend
And I am lucky
Between the calm and the calamity
Lies the beauty
The artistic and the altruistic
Human duty; I'm in for a pound
Yet finally unbound, I am free
To be fairly optimistic
After all
I am so lucky.

Morning Light

As light dances across the room we share
You smile your love on me
Gently waking us to one more day spent together
How many we have, I wonder
Burying my head in your shoulder
I try not to think of a day
When I may wake alone
But you breathe hope on me
And gaze at me with your clear blue love
I don't like knowing that you own my heart
That you could hurt me irrevocably
Pushing away the fear
Because I know you feel the same
So I will live in this moment
As light dances across the room we share

Alive

I am alive
Once merely lingering, undeniably
Through the journey I have thrived
Pain dwells in me
Eight swords still mark the space
But blinded, I am bound
To this time and place
I am alive
The searing burn inside
Recognizes the offense
An ache that won't subside
But still I am alive
The recompense is joy
Laughter that resides
Deep down, a place I thought destroyed
It's true; I am alive
Excitement of uncertain futures
The Wheel of Fortune turns
Rumors in the cards discerned
Afflicted by the Sword
With dreams that have yet to die
Yes, I am alive
An unlikely state from past mistakes
The Hanged Man now is loved
A Lover, he becomes
Beholden, he succumbs
Driven to survive
Indeed, I am alive

Drifting down a nameless road
The signs of life abound
A Fool's errand, I know
All around me, a presage
I am a life compelled
A glimmer, just a vestige
The hidden hazards of the Moon
In the Sun dispelled
Still Death, a knight, rides close
Morose, I journey forward
Simply because I am alive
A portent of the end of days
But days till then I'll spend
With Justice, who sits on her throne
Her sword alone is raised
This is the company I keep
The path I have embraced
While still I am alive
Further down the quiet road
I stride in hopes to find
A way to lift the load
To fix the broken kind
The chaos in the sky
Death about to die
I'll doctor it the best I can
And breathe into it life
For all around the signs are there
And I am still alive

Appendix

Sources for "Endless Night" Footnotes
1. Milton, John. *Paradise Lost*. Cutchogue, New York: Buccaneer Books, Inc., 1976.
2. Thomas, Dylan. "Fern Hill." *The Norton Anthology of English Literature, Vol. 2*. Edited by M.H. Abrams. New York: W.W. Norton & Company, 1993. 2284-85.
3. Marvell, Andrew. "To His Coy Mistress." *The Norton Anthology of English Literature, Vol. 1*. Edited by M.H. Abrams. New York: W.W. Norton & Company, 1993. 1420-21.
4. Shakespeare, William. *Hamlet. The Complete Works of William Shakespeare*. Edited by Arthur Henry Bullen. New York: Dorset Press, 1988. Act. I, scene V, line 14, p. 677.
5. Poe, Edgar Allen. "The Raven." *The Complete Works of Edgar Allen Poe*. USA: Crown Publishers, 1985. 708.
6. Wells, H.G. *The Island of Dr. Moreau. The Complete Works of H.G. Wells*. USA: Crown Publishers, 1979. 154.
7. Marvell, Andrew. "To His Coy Mistress." *The Norton Anthology of English Literature, Vol. 1*. Edited by M.H. Abrams. New York: W.W. Norton & Company, 1993. 1420-21.
8. Bronte, Emily. *Wuthering Heights*. Edited by David Daiches. London: Penguin Books, 1993. 67.
9. Smith, Stevie. "The New Age." *The Norton Anthology of English Literature, Vol. 2*. Edited by M.H. Abrams. New York: W.W. Norton & Company, 1993. 2223-24.
10. Plato's "Allegory of the Cave." P. Shorey trans. from *Plato: Collected Dialogues*, eds. Hamilton and Cairns. Random House, 1963.
11. Doyle, Sir Arthur Conan. "The Hound of the Baskervilles." *The Complete Works of Sir Arthur Conan Doyle*. USA: Crown Publishers, 1984. 535.
12. Bradbury, Ray. *Something Wicked This Way Comes*. New York: Bantam Books, Inc., 1962.
13. Rosetti, Christina. "The Goblin Market." *The Norton Anthology of English Literature, Vol. 2*. Edited by M.H. Abrams. New York: W.W. Norton & Company, 1993. 1479.
14. Doyle, Sir Arthur Conan. "The Hound of the Baskervilles." *The Complete Works of Sir Arthur Conan Doyle*. USA: Crown Publishers, 1984. 535.
15. Heaney, Seamus. "Station Island." *The Norton Anthology of English Literature, Vol. 2*. Edited by M.H. Abrams. New York: W.W. Norton & Company, 1993. 2428-30.
16. Yeats, William Butler. "Easter 1916." *The Norton Anthology of English*

Literature, Vol. 2. Edited by M.H. Abrams. New York: W.W. Norton & Company, 1993. 1880.
17. Spenser, Edmund. "The Faerie Queen." *The Norton Anthology of English Literature*, Vol. 1. Edited by M.H. Abrams. New York: W.W. Norton & Company, 1993. 1517, I.i.13.
18. Poe, Edgar Allen. "The Raven." *The Complete Works of Edgar Allen Poe*. USA: Crown Publishers, 1985. 708.
19. Tolkien, J.R.R. *The Hobbit*. New York: Ballantine Books, 1973. 78.
20. Tolkien, J.R.R. *The Hobbit*. New York: Ballantine Books, 1973. 76.
21. *The NIV Study Bible*. Edited by Kenneth Barker. Grand Rapids: Zondervan Bible Publishers, 1985. Psalm 91:6.
22. Eliot, T.S. "The Love Song of Alfred J. Prufrock." *The Norton Anthology of English Literature*, Vol. 2. Edited by M.H. Abrams. New York: W.W. Norton & Company, 1993. 2142.
23. Yeats, William Butler. "Easter 1916." *The Norton Anthology of English Literature*, Vol. 2. Edited by M.H. Abrams. New York: W.W. Norton & Company, 1993. 1879.
24. Plato's "Allegory of the Cave." P. Shorey *trans. from Plato: Collected Dialogues*, eds. Hamilton and Cairns. Random House, 1963.
25. *The NIV Study Bible*. Edited by Kenneth Barker. Grand Rapids: Zondervan Bible Publishers, 1985. Proverbs 4:19.
26. Shakespeare, William. "Sonnet 29." *The Complete Works of William Shakespeare*. Edited by Arthur Henry Bullen. New York: Dorset Press, 1988. 811.
27. Wells, H.G. *The Island of Dr. Moreau*. *The Complete Works of H.G. Wells*. USA: Crown Publishers, 1979. 154.
28. Eliot, T.S. "The Love Song of Alfred J. Prufrock." *The Norton Anthology of English Literature*, Vol. 2. Edited by M.H. Abrams. New York: W.W. Norton & Company, 1993. 2140.
29. *The NIV Study Bible*. Edited by Kenneth Barker. Grand Rapids: Zondervan Bible Publishers, 1985. Genesis 6:13.
30. Milton, John. "L'Allegro." *The Norton Anthology of English Literature*, Vol. 1. Edited by M.H. Abrams. New York: W.W. Norton & Company, 1993. 1443.
31. Shakespeare, William. "Sonnet 29." *The Complete Works of William Shakespeare*. Edited by Arthur Henry Bullen. New York: Dorset Press, 1988. 811.
32. *The NIV Study Bible*. Edited by Kenneth Barker. Grand Rapids: Zondervan Bible Publishers, 1985. Psalm 119:105.
33. Yeats, William Butler. "The Lake Isle of Innisfree." *The Norton Anthology of English Literature*, Vol. 2. Edited by M.H. Abrams. New York: W.W. Norton & Company, 1993. 1867.
34. Thomas, Dylan. "Do Not Go Gentle Into That Good Night." *The*

Norton Anthology of English Literature, Vol. 2. Edited by M.H. Abrams. New York: W.W. Norton & Company, 1993. 2286.

About the Author

Christina Knowles is the author of the suspense thriller, *The Ezekiel Project*, as well as publishing two weekly blogs, disturbingtheuniverseblog.com and secularbohemian.com. In addition to writing, she teaches creative writing, composition, and literature on both the high school and the college level in Colorado Springs, where she resides with her husband, musician Randy Knowles, and her dog, Chacho. She is currently working on a collection of haunting stories as well as a new mystery-suspense thriller.

Also by Christina Knowles

The Ezekiel Project, A Novel

She knows a secret; he knows the future. Together they will expose the truth.

A young mother risks everything to expose a top-secret government project with the help of its most important test subject, a dying Gulf War veteran with paranormal abilities . . . Eleven years after the bombing of his battalion in Iraq, Joel's nightmares continue. But when a beautiful young mother enters those dreams, he knows he must do everything in his power to save her from those who want to silence her, including stopping the man responsible for his nightmares, her husband, and the man who has been keeping him prisoner in a top-secret government facility in charge of The Ezekiel Project.

"*The Ezekiel Project* by debut author, Christina Knowles--Wow, this was a ride and a half! A fast-paced, interesting, thought provoking, edge-of-your-seat story about clandestine military medical experimentation, telekinesis, mind control, abuse, and love. Knowles is a master of pacing... Impossible to put down ... highly recommend ... This just-released suspense novel is a sleep-robbing page-turner!" --Lee Fullbright, award winning author of *The Angry Woman Suite*.

Paperback and Kindle Edition available on Amazon.com

www.ingramcontent.com/pod-product-compliance
Lightning Source LLC
LaVergne TN
LVHW091301080426
835510LV00007B/352